Wailing Winny's car bo

Story written by Gill Munton
Illustrated by Tim Archbold

Speed Sounds

Consonants   *Ask children to say the sounds.*

f	l	m	n	r	s	v	z	sh	th	**ng**
ff	ll	mm	nn	rr	ss	ve	zz			nk
ph	le	mb	kn	wr	se		se			
			gn		c		s			
					ce					

b	c	d	g	h	j	p	qu	t	w	x	y	ch
bb	k	dd	gg		**g**	pp		tt	wh			tch
	ck		gu		ge							

Each box contains one sound but sometimes more than one grapheme.
*Focus graphemes for this story are **circled**.*

4

Vowels   *Ask children to say the sounds in and out of order.*

a	e ea	i	o	u	ay a-e a ai aigh	ee ea e y	igh i-e ie i y	ow o-e oa o oe

oo u-e ue ew	oo	ar	or oor ore aw	air are	ir ur er	ou ow	oy oi	ire	ear

Story Green Words

Ask children to read the words first in Fred Talk and then say the word.

Spain   sale   crate   slime   pale   drain   chain   faint

Ask children to say the syllables and then read the whole word.

bar|gain   fing|er|nails   train|ers   pea|brain

Ask children to read the root first and then the whole word with the suffix.

exclaim → exclaimed   straighten → straightening   peer → peered

contain → containing   complain → complained   rev → revving

nail → nailed   trail → trailed   raise → raised

demonstrate → demonstrating   ghost → ghostly*

* Challenge Words

6

Vocabulary Check

Discuss the meaning (as used in the story) after the children have read each word.

	definition:	sentence:
bargain	*something that is cheap or really good value*	*Lots of bargains!*
crate	*box*	*A crate containing old toenail clippings*
cash	*money*	*I'll take the cash straight to the Banshee Bank.*
revving up	*starting up*	*"I'll try and get them back," wailed Winny, revving up her broomstick.*
down the drain	*wasted*	*That was £2.50 down the drain!*
demonstrating	*showing*	*"Yes! I've turned them into sparkly sandals," exclaimed Nelly, demonstrating with her magic wand.*

Red Words

Ask children to practise reading the words across the rows, down the columns and in and out of order clearly and quickly.

buy	bought	do	some
to	of	said	you
bought	some	what	father
mother	son	here	come
could	should	through	any

Wailing Winny's car boot sale

Winny stuck the poster to the wall of her cave with a blob of bat spit.

"Perfect!" she exclaimed, straightening her pointy hat.

Car Boot Sale!
Today in the Snailtrail Cave!
Lots of bargains!

Winny peered into the boot of her witchmobile,
ticking things off on her long fingernails:

- a book of out-of-date spells
  (a bit stained)
- a set of second-hand chains
- a crate containing old
  toenail clippings
- six cans of snail slime
- a rat's tail
  oh yes, and
- a pair of smelly old trainers

All Winny's mates came to the boot sale, and everything was sold.

"I'll take the cash straight to the Banshee Bank,"
said Winny's husband, Phantom Phil.
"Have you seen my trainers?"

You Peabrain!

"Trainers!" Winny gulped.

"Winny! You peabrain!
You've sold my best trainers!"
Phil complained, swishing round the
cave in a rage.

"I'll try and get them back," wailed Winny, revving up her broomstick.

First, she paid a visit to Chilly Charly's coffin. The lid creaked open and Charly's pale face poked out.

"Did you buy a pair of smelly old trainers at the boot sale?" wailed Winny.

"I'm afraid not!" complained Charly. "I bought the book of out-of-date spells — and I paid £2.50 for it! (That was £2.50 down the drain!)"

Winny nailed his lid down again.

Next, she visited Sam the Spook's attic.
Ghostly fingers trailed past Winny's face.

"Wait! Did you buy a pair of smelly
old trainers at the boot sale?"
she wailed.

"I'm afraid not!" hooted Sam. "I bought the chains –
I'm doing them up for Hallowe'en!"
He faded away.

Winny raised the rusty lid of the dustbin.
Dustbin Dave crouched in an old paint tin
among the marmalade jars and cake crumbs.

"Is it dustbin day?" he grunted.

"No!" wailed Winny.
"Did you buy a pair of smelly old trainers
at the boot sale?"

"Not me," grunted Dave. "I bought the toenail clippings –
I've always wanted some!" He waved, and banged down the lid.

Smelly Nelly was sitting on a pile of rubbish in the rain.

"Did you buy a pair of smelly old trainers at the boot sale?" wailed Winny.

"Yes! I've turned them into sparkly sandals for my holiday in Spain!" explained Nelly, demonstrating with her magic wand.

Winny felt faint. "Well, you'd better turn them back again!"

Nelly waved a pair of dusty lace-up boots in Winny's face.
"Will these do instead?" she grinned.
"I'm having a boot sale of my own –
and I'm selling these boots!
A bargain at £500!"

Questions to talk about

Ask children to TTYP each question using 'Fastest finger' (FF) or 'Have a think' (HaT).

p.9 (FF) What did Winny use to stick the poster to the wall?

p.10 (FF) What was the last thing on Winny's list?

p.11 (HaT) Why did Winny gulp when Phil asked about his trainers?

p.12 (FF) What did Charly buy from the car boot sale?

p.13 (FF) What did Sam buy from the car boot sale?

p.13 (FF) What did Dave buy from the car boot sale?

p.13 (HaT) Do you think Nelly's boots are a bargain?

Questions to read and answer

(Children complete without your help.)

1. Where does Winny have her car boot sale?

2. What did Winny sell that belonged to her husband?

3. Why did Sam buy the chains?

4. Why did Smelly Nelly buy the pair of smelly old trainers?

5. What does Smelly Nelly mean when she says she is having a boot sale?

Speedy Green Words

straight	everything	face	afraid
complained	magic	these	take
round	first	having	always
instead	straight	everything	face
afraid	long	complained	magic